THE ULTIMATE
FOOTBALL
FACT BOOK

FOR KIDS

Broadwood Press are an independent publishing team that aims to provide fun and educational books for young readers.

All facts within this book are accurate at the time of publishing. However, if you happen to spot anything that needs to be corrected, please email us at **broadwoodpress@gmail.com** and we will be more than happy to help you out.

ISBN: 9798864169155

FREE COLORING PAGES!!

Scan the QR code below to download some bonus football coloring pages to carry on the fun!!

1.

The first college football game between Rutgers and Princeton in 1869 had 25 players per side and used a round ball.

2.

The Green Bay Packers have won more NFL championships than any other team.

3.

American football had a 55-yard line until 1912.

4.

Michigan Stadium, also known as the "Big House," seats 107,601 fans and is the largest college football stadium.

5.

Eric Dickerson set the NFL record for most rushing yards in a season with 2,105 in 1984.

6.

Peyton Manning set the NFL record for most passing yards in a season with 5,477 in 2013.

7.

Ray Guy is the only punter in the Pro Football Hall of Fame.

8.

Two founding member NFL teams are still in the league: the Decatur Staleys (now the Chicago Bears) and the Chicago Cardinals (now the Arizona Cardinals).

9.

The smallest NFL stadium is Soldier Field in Chicago. It seats only 61,500 people.

10.

According to the NCAA, the two college football teams with the most national championships are Yale and Alabama..

11.

The first Heisman Trophy winner was Jay Berwanger of the University of Chicago (1935).

12.

Archie Griffin of Ohio State is the only two-time Heisman Trophy winner. He won in 1974 and 1975.

13.
The most popular team colors in the NFL are blue, black, and red.

14.
"Tigers" is the most popular team nickname among major college (FBS) football teams. Auburn, Clemson, LSU, Memphis, and Missouri are the Tigers.

15.
Michigan is the most successful college football team in history.

16.
The end zone is 10-yards deep in American football and is 20-yards deep in Canadian football.

17.

Early football was played with a ball made with an inflated pig bladder. That is why the football is called the pigskin.

18.

Football fields are 53 1/3 yards or 160 feet wide.

19.

The forward pass was legalized in 1906 and was first thrown in a regulation game by Bradbury Robinson of St. Louis University.

20.

AT&T Stadium, the home of the Dallas Cowboys, is the largest in the NFL, with a capacity of 100,000 people.

21.

The fullback was the player who stood farthest from the ball in early football. Players who stood half as far from the ball were halfbacks, and the player who stood only one-quarter of the way back became the quarterback.

22.

The NFL and NCAA footballs must weigh between 14 and 15 ounces.

23.

Mike Hart of Michigan carried the ball 1,005 consecutive times without fumbling.

24.

In 2016, Patrick Mahomes set the NCAA record for total offense in a game at 819 yards.

25.
The college (FBS) record for most points in a season is 236, set by Montee Ball of Wisconsin in 2011.

26.
Many consider the 1958 NFL Championship game between the Baltimore Colts and New York Giants to be "The Greatest Game Ever Played."

27.
The first Super Bowl was played on January 15, 1967. The Green Bay Packers beat the Kansas Chiefs 35-10.

28.
The most-played college football rivalry is the Lehigh-Lafayette series.

29.

NFL and NCAA goal posts are 18 feet 6 inches wide. High school goal posts are 23 feet 4 inches wide.

30.

The first football player to have his number retired was Red Grange. He wore Number 77 for the University of Illinois between 1923 and 1925.

31.

Walter Camp helped define many early football rules and was a successful player and coach at Yale.

32.

Because of this, Walter Camp is known as "The Father of Football."

33.
The Seattle Seahawks are the NFL's northmost and westernmost team.

34.
The New England Patriots are the NFL's easternmost team, and the Miami Dolphins are the southernmost team.

35.
The NFL first required visiting teams to wear white jerseys in 1957, which helped television viewers distinguish the team on the black-and-white televisions of the era.

36.
The NCAA did not require players to wear face masks until 1993.

37.
Tom Brady led the New England Patriots to nine Super Bowls and six Super Bowl wins.

38.
The 1972 Miami Dolphins were the only NFL team to go undefeated in the regular season and postseason, going 17-0.

39.
The Buffalo Bills and Minnesota Vikings have 0-4 records in the Super Bowl.

40.
George Blanda played an NFL record 26 seasons as a quarterback and kicker.

41.

Jason Hanson holds the NFL record for the most seasons played with the same team. He played 21 seasons with the Detroit Lions.

42.

Joe Thomas holds the NFL record for most consecutive snaps at 10,363.

43.

Jerry Rice holds the NFL record for most career touchdowns, with 208.

44.

Rob Bironas of the Tennessee Titans made eight field goals in one game in 2007 without a miss.

45.
The NFL record for the longest field goal is 66 yards, set by Justin Tucker of the Detroit Lions in 2021.

46.
Drew Bledsoe attempted an NFL record 70 passes in one game in 1994.

47.
Paul Krause, who played for the Minnesota Vikings and Washington Redskins from 1964 to 1979, holds the NFL record for most interceptions in a career at 81.

48.
Football's first helmet logo appeared on the University of Chicago helmets in 1921.

49.
The Los Angeles Rams wore the NFL's first helmet logos in 1948.

50.
The first NCAA overtime game came in the 1976 Division 3 playoffs when Upper Iowa beat Carroll University.

51.
Football officials first used whistles in 1887. Many officials used horns and bells until the 1950s.

52.
Youngstown State coach Dwight "Dike" Beede invented the penalty flag in 1941.

53.

The NCAA officially adopted penalty flags in 1948.

54.

Woodrow Wilson, Dwight Eisenhower, and Gerald Ford coached college football before they became U.S. President.

55.

American football fields did not have end zones until 1912.

56.

A pancake block occurs when an offensive lineman knocks an opposing player to the ground and lands on top of them.

57.
Lloyd W. Olds, a professor at Eastern Michigan, invented the black-and-white striped officials' shirt in the early 1920s.

58.
The first American football games in Mexico came in 1896 when the Universities of Missouri and Texas played in Mexico City and Monterrey.

59.
Touchdowns did not earn more points than field goals until 1904.

60.
Football teams had three downs to gain five yards until 1906.

61.

Until the 1950s, teams often used balls painted white or yellow for night games.

62.

The Olympics included football as a test sport during the 1904 and 1932 games.

63.

The American Football Statistical Bureau, an independent company, began gathering consistent college football statistics in 1937.

64.

The NCAA acquired "The American Football Statistical Bureau" in the late 1950s.

65.
The University of North Carolina became the first Southern team to play in the North when it played Lehigh in Manhattan in 1893.

66.
Football players began wearing eye black in the early 1940s.

67.
To protest the requirement to wear uniform numbers, some teams wore four-digit numbers or Roman numerals.

68.
The Hec Crighton Award honors Canada's top college football player.

69.

The 1904 All-American team had ten players from Yale on the first or second team.

70.

The first shoulder pads were small leather pads sewn on the jersey exterior.

71.

Princeton's T. H. Harris recovered a fumble and ran it the field's length in a game versus Lafayette in 1883 for the first documented scoop-and-score.

72.

Football cheerleading was an all-male activity until Elizabeth Morrow led the University of Kansas women in 1913.

73.

The first face masks appeared in the 1920s.

74.

Football chains were invented in 1894 by members of the Crescent Athletic Club in Brooklyn.

75.

"The Star-Spangled Banner" was first played shortly before football games in 1917.

76.

Jackie Robinson was a star football player at UCLA before becoming the first African American player in major league baseball.

77.

Georgia Tech was the first team to play in the Rose Bowl, Sugar Bowl, Orange Bowl, and Cotton Bowl.

78.

Stripes first started appearing on footballs in the 1950s.

79.

The Kentucky School for the Blind fielded a football team in the 1910s, playing teams with sighted players under modified rules.

80.

Great Britain's Queen Elizabeth II attended the 1957 North Carolina vs Maryland football game.

81.
The 1921 Illinois team was the first to huddle during games consistently.

82.
Georgia, Notre Dame, Oklahoma, and USC have each had at least five players selected as #1 in the NFL Draft.

83.
Yale's Wyllys Terry had a 115-yard touchdown run in 1884.

84.
Until 1926, the football remained live when it went out of bounds.

85.

Four schools that do not currently play FBS football have had players drafted as #1 in the NFL draft.

86.

These are Tennessee State, Tampa, the University of Pennsylvania, and the University of Chicago.

87.

In 2019, Joe Burrow set the NCAA FBS record for most total yards in a season with 6,040.

88.

Case Keenum of Houston (2007-2011) passed for 19,217 yards in his career.

89.
Levell Coppage of Wisconsin-Whitewater had 1,324 rushing attempts in his career, the most for an NCAA player at any level.

90.
Coppage also holds the record for most career games of 100 or more yards rushing (42).

91.
The FBS record for the highest rushing average per game in a career is 174.6 yards, held by Ed Marinaro.

92.
Andre Ware of Houston threw for 340 yards in one quarter and 517 yards in one half during a 1989 game.

93.

David Klingler of Houston threw 11 touchdown passes in a game versus Eastern Washington in 1990.

94.

John Reaves threw nine interceptions in a college football game for Florida in 1969.

95.

Washington holds the NCAA record for the longest unbeaten streak at 64 (60-0-4), set between 1907 and 1917.

96.

Oklahoma holds the record for most consecutive wins at 47, set between 1953 and 1957.

97.

Miami holds the record for most consecutive wins at home at 58, set between 1985 and 1994.

98.

Northwestern holds the record for most consecutive losses at 34, set between 1979 and 1982.

99.

Don Shula won a staggering 328 matches as an NFL coach.

100.

Thanks to these wins, Don Shula had an NFL win percentage of 67.7%.

101.
The NFL roster limit was 16 in 1925.

102.
Two NFL teams, the San Francisco 49ers and the Cleveland Browns, began as members of the rival All-America Football Conference in 1946.

103.
The Green Bay Packers have won more NFL matches than any other team in history.

104.
In contrast, the Houston Texans have recorded the fewest wins.

105.
Three of the five NFL games with the highest-paid attendance were played in Mexico.

106.
Almost 19 million people attended NFL games in 2022.

107.
Pudge Heffelfinger became the first professional football player when he accepted $500 to play in a game for the Allegheny Athletic Association in 1892.

108.
The Pro Football Hall of Fame includes more than 350 inductees.

109.
The Latrobe Athletic Association was the first team to play a full season as a fully professional team in 1897.

110.
The Akron Pros won the first NFL championship in 1920.

111.
The Green Bay Packers and Chicago Bears have played each other more often than any other NFL teams.

112.
The New England Patriots have played in more Super Bowl matches than any other team.

113.
The NFL's Monday Night Football premiered in 1970.

114.
The NFL's first Thanksgiving games were held in 1920.

115.
The NFL record for the most receptions in a game is 21, set by Brandon Marshall in December 2009.

116.
The NFL record for the most receiving yards in a game is 303, set by Jim Benton of the Cleveland Rams in 1945.

117.
The Cleveland Browns are the only NFL team not to decorate its helmets with a logo.

118.
The NFL Man of the Year Award recognizes an active player for his community involvement.

119.
Peyton Manning is the only player to receive the NFL MVP Award five times.

120.
Jim Brown won the NFL MVP Award two times and is the only non-quarterback to win the award more than once.

121.
Alan Page won the NFL's first Associated Press Defensive Player of the Year Award in 1971.

122.
O.J. Simpson won the NFL's first Associated Press Offensive Player of the Year Award in 1973.

123.
Quarterbacks have been the NFL's #1 draft choice more times than any other position.

124.
The next most popular position to be drafted #1 is running back.

125.

The NFL had 32 rounds in the draft from 1943 to 1948.

126.

The NFL playoffs include the four division winners and two "wild card" teams from each conference.

127.

The NFL implemented a new rule in 2011 that moved kickoffs from the 30-yard line to the 35-yard line to reduce high-speed collisions.

128.

Morten Andersen played in an NFL record 382 games between 1982 and 2007.

129.
The Baltimore Ravens are named after Edgar Allan Poe's poem, "The Raven."

130.
The Chicago Bears began as the Decatur Staleys but adopted the Bears name to be consistent with baseball's Chicago Cubs.

131.
The Los Angeles Rams originated in Cleveland.

132.

The National Football League (NFL) was founded in 1920 as the American Professional Football Association (APFA) and adopted its current name in 1922.

133.

The Super Bowl, the NFL championship game, is one of the most-watched sporting events in the United States.

134.

The Vince Lombardi Trophy is awarded to the Super Bowl winner, named after the legendary Green Bay Packers coach.

135.

Walter Payton holds the record for the most career rushing yards in the NFL, with 16,726.

136.

NFL teams are divided into the American Football Conference (AFC) and the National Football Conference (NFC).

137.
The NFL has a draft and salary cap system to promote competitive team balance.

138.
The NFL Draft is an annual event where NFL teams select college players.

139.
During the draft, teams choose players in reverse order of the previous season's standings.

140.
The first televised football game in which an instant replay was used was the 1963 Army-Navy game.

141.

The "Hail Mary" is a term used to describe a long, last-ditch pass attempt to the end zone, often at the end of a game.

142.

Steve O'Neal had the longest punt in NFL history in 1969. It traveled 98 yards.

143.

The NFL Scouting Combine is an event where draft-eligible players undergo physical and mental evaluations before NFL team representatives.

144.

The Kansas City Chiefs' Arrowhead Stadium is known for having a loud fan base, often called the "Sea of Red."

145.

"Hail Flutie" is a famous play where quarterback Doug Flutie threw a game-winning touchdown pass for Boston College against Miami in 1984.

146.

The Chicago Bears are known as the "Monsters of the Midway."

147.

The New York Jets won their only Super Bowl in 1969.

148.

The Green Bay Packers are the only community-owned franchise in the NFL.

149.
The "No Fun League" is a nickname some fans use to criticize the NFL for its strict rules and penalties on celebrations.

150.
The NFL has an "Injured Reserve" list for players who cannot participate for several weeks due to injuries.

151.
The St. Louis Rams won Super Bowl XXXIV in 2000 with a team known as the "Greatest Show on Turf."

152.
The Buffalo Bills played in four consecutive Super Bowls from 1990 to 1993 but did not win any of them.

153.
The Indianapolis Colts moved from Baltimore to Indianapolis in 1984.

154.
The Detroit Lions traditionally play on Thanksgiving Day, which dates to 1934.

155.
The NFL's "franchise tag" mechanism allows teams to retain one player per year who would otherwise become a free agent.

156.
The Heisman Trophy is awarded to the best college football player in the United States.

157.

The Heisman Trophy is among the most prestigious individual awards in the sport.

158.

The Rose Bowl is among the most iconic postseason college football games and is the oldest.

159.

It is held in Pasadena, California, on New Year's Day.

160.

The Iron Bowl, played between the University of Alabama and Auburn University, is among the fiercest rivalry games in college football.

161.

Notre Dame Stadium, home to the Notre Dame Fighting Irish, is known for its "Touchdown Jesus" mural and rich football history.

162.

The University of Michigan's stadium is known as "The Big House."

163.

It got its name because it has a capacity of over 100,000.

164.

Boise State's "Statue of Liberty" play, executed in the 2007 Fiesta Bowl, is among college football's most famous trick plays.

165.

College football is known for its rich traditions, including marching bands, fight songs, and unique mascots.

166.

Nick Saban, the coach at Alabama, won one national championship while coaching LSU.

167.

The Big Ten Conference was founded in 1896 with seven schools.

168.

These schools were Chicago, Illinois, Michigan, Minnesota, Northwestern, Purdue, and Wisconsin.

169.

The "Little Brown Jug" is a trophy awarded to the winner of the Michigan versus Minnesota game and is among the oldest college football trophies.

170.

The "Old Oaken Bucket" is a trophy contested between Indiana and Purdue.

171.

An Ohio State Buckeyes band tradition is "dotting the 'i'" in their Script Ohio formation during halftime.

172.

The University of Chicago was a founding member of the Big Ten but withdrew from the conference in 1946.

173.

The "Paul Bunyan's Axe" trophy is awarded to the Minnesota vs. Wisconsin game-winner.

174.

Michigan's fight song, "The Victors" was composed in 1898 by Louis Elbel following a victory over the University of Chicago.

175.

The Southeastern Conference (SEC) was founded in 1932.

176.

The SEC is considered to be the most competitive conference in college football.

177.

The Paul "Bear" Bryant Award is given annually to the nation's top college football coach.

178.

Florida's stadium is called "The Swamp" and is one of college football's loudest and most intimidating stadiums.

179.

The annual game between Ole Miss and Mississippi State is called the "Egg Bowl."

180.

The Pac-12 Conference was founded in 1915 as the Pacific Coast Conference (PCC).

181.

The "Apple Cup" is the rivalry game between Washington State and Washington.

182.

Washington's "Husky Stadium" is known for its picturesque location on the shores of Lake Washington.

183.

The Atlantic Coast Conference (ACC) was founded in 1953.

184.

The ACC initially included Clemson, Duke, Maryland, North Carolina, North Carolina State, South Carolina, and Wake Forest.

185.

"Frank Howard Field at Clemson Memorial Stadium" is among college football's loudest and most intimidating stadiums.

186.

It's home to the Clemson Tigers and is nicknamed "Death Valley".

187.

Virginia Military Institute (VMI) and The Citadel play the "Military Classic of the South" rivalry game.

188.

The Ivy League consists of eight private institutions in the northeastern United States.

189.
These institutions are Brown, Columbia, Cornell, Dartmouth, Harvard, Penn, Princeton, and Yale.

190.
The Harvard-Yale football game, known as "The Game," is among college football's oldest and most famous rivalries.

191.
The Ivy League does not participate in the FCS playoffs.

192.
Instead, they determine their conference champion based on the regular-season standings.

193.
The Ivy League does not allow athletic scholarships or redshirting, so their student-athletes typically complete their football eligibility in four years.

194.
The three-way rivalry among Harvard, Yale, and Princeton were major forces in shaping early football.

195.
The Big 12 has been known for its innovative offensive schemes and pass-heavy game plans.

196.
The first NFL game was played on October 3, 1920, between the Dayton Triangles and the Columbus Panhandles.

197.
Fritz Pollard was the NFL's first African American head coach in 1921.

198.
The Denver Broncos have the longest sellout streak in the NFL, which began in 1970.

199.
The first Super Bowl halftime show featured college marching bands, not famous musical acts.

200.
The NFL officially began using instant replay for officiating reviews in 1986.

201.

The longest winning streak in NFL history belongs to the Indianapolis Colts, who won 23 consecutive games from 2008 and 2009.

202.

The longest home winning streak in the NFL belongs to the Miami Dolphins, who won 27 games between 1971 and 1974.

203.

The longest away winning streak in NFL history belongs to the San Francisco 49ers, who won 18 games between 1988 and 1990.

204.

The Detroit Lions have never appeared in a Super Bowl.

205.
The NFL banned using "stickum," a sticky substance used by players to improve grip, in 1981.

206.
Wilson Sporting Goods is the official supplier of footballs to the NFL.

207.
Peyton Manning became the first quarterback to win a Super Bowl with two different teams (Indianapolis Colts in 2007 and Denver Broncos in 2016).

208.
Calvin Johnson, known as "Megatron," set the single-season receiving yards record with 1,964 yards in 2012.

209.

The NFL held its first regular-season game in London in 2007 when the Miami Dolphins played the New York Giants at Wembley Stadium.

210.

The NFL expanded to 32 teams by adding the Houston Texans in 2002.

211.

The NFL earned approximately $11.9 billion in revenue in 2022, with each team receiving around $370 million.

212.

In 2017, the Atlanta Falcons had a 28-3 lead in Super Bowl LI but lost to the Patriots 34-28 in overtime.

213.

Adrian Peterson gained 2,097 rushing yards in 2012, just 8 yards shy of breaking Eric Dickerson's single-season rushing record of 2,105.

214.

The Rams were in Cleveland from 1936 through 1945 before moving to LA.

215.

They then moved to St. Louis in 1995 and remained there until 2016.

216.

The Oakland Raiders joined the AFL in 1960, moved to Los Angeles in 1982, and returned to Oakland in 1995 before relocating to Las Vegas in 2020.

217.

The NFL introduced the "Rooney Rule" in 2002 to promote diversity in coaching and executive positions.

218.

The NFL had its first female official, Sarah Thomas, in 2015.

219.

NFL players embrace social justice initiatives, including kneeling during the national anthem, which began in 2016.

220.

The New Orleans Saints were temporarily displaced due to Hurricane Katrina in 2005.

221.
During this time, they played one home game at the New York Giants' home field and other games at LSU and the Alamodome in San Antonio.

222.
The University of Southern California (USC) won consecutive national championships in 2003 and 2004.

223.
Johnny Manziel, also known as "Johnny Football," won the Heisman Trophy in 2012 as a freshman at Texas A&M.

224.
The FBS level of college football has seen regular conference realignment in the last two decades.

225.

The Georgia-Florida game played in Jacksonville, Florida, is known as the "World's Largest Outdoor Cocktail Party."

226.

The Texas A&M Aggies joined the Southeastern Conference (SEC) in 2012.

227.

Tom Brady holds the NFL records for career passing yards, completed passes, and touchdown passes.

228.

The NFL's career-leading rusher is Emmitt Smith, with 18,355 yards.

229.

Jerry Rice holds the NFL record for career yards from scrimmage at 23,540.

230.

The NFL's career leader for kick return average is Gale Sayers, with an average of 30.6.

231.

Bruce Smith recorded 200 sacks in his career.

232.

Bill Belichick has coached in nine Super Bowls and has won six, both NFL records.

233.
James White scored 20 points in Super Bowl LI.

234.
Jim Turner of the New York Jets attempted six field goals in Super Bowl III, and the Cowboys' Efren Herrera did the same in Super Bowl XII.

235.
Franco Harris holds the Super Bowl record for career rushing attempts (101) and yards gained (354).

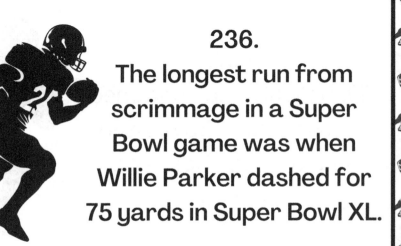

236.
The longest run from scrimmage in a Super Bowl game was when Willie Parker dashed for 75 yards in Super Bowl XL.

237.
John Elway threw a record eight interceptions in five Super Bowl games.

238.
Green Bay quarterback Bart Starr was the MVP of Super Bowls I and II.

239.
Detroit and Minneapolis have hosted two Super Bowls, each holding them in two different stadiums.

240.
Players on the winning team received $157,000 for Super Bowl LVII versus $15,000 for Super Bowl I.

241.

The NFL Pro Bowl began in 1939, and the first five games had an all-star team play the NFL champs.

242.

The first overtime game in NFL history was an exhibition game between the Los Angeles Rams and the New Giants.

243.

The Los Angeles Rams won the game 23-17.

244.

The NFL's first regular-season overtime game between the Steelers and Broncos ended in a 35-35 tie on September 22, 1974.

245.
The NFL's shortest overtime game came in a 2012 Wild Card playoff game when Denver beat Pittsburgh in 11 seconds.

246.
The Cleveland Browns beat the New York Jets 31-21 in the first-ever Monday Night Football game on September 21, 1970.

247.
The NFL named all-decades teams from the 1920s to the 2010s.

248.
The NFL's first Sunday Night Football game came in 1978 when New England beat Oakland 21-14.

249.

Three players on the NFL's All-1920s team played for the Great Lakes Naval Training Station team during WWI.

250.

These players were George Halas, Paddy Driscoll, and Jimmy Conzelman.

251.

After a fair catch, teams can attempt an uncontested field goal from the spot of the fair catch.

252.

The Outland Trophy, named after coach John Outland, goes to the best interior lineman in the country.

253.

The Doak Walker Award goes to the nation's top running back. Walker played for SMU from 1945 to 1949.

254.

The Butkus Award is named after Dick Butkus and goes to the top linebacker in college football.

255.

The Burlsworth Award goes to the nation's top former walk-on.

256.

The award is named after Brandon Burlsworth, a walk-on at Arkansas who became an All-American.

257.

The award for the nation's top college coach is the Eddie Robinson Award, named after Grambling's long-time head coach.

258.

An audible is a play called at the line of scrimmage by the quarterback.

259.

A blitz occurs when a defensive player who typically stays on his side of the line of scrimmages attempts to break into the offensive backfield after the snap.

260.

Previously called a "red dog", "blitz" became the preferred term in the late 1950s.

261.

A bootleg occurs when a quarterback fakes the ball to a back running in one direction and takes the ball in the opposite direction.

262.

Pop Warner's Stanford teams ran the first bootleg in the 1920s.

263.

The center is an offensive lineman that aligns over the ball and snaps it to the quarterback or a running back.

264.

The center was originally called the snapper-back.

265.

Cornerbacks are defensive players that align on the outside with the primary responsibility to cover pass plays.

266.

The Pac-12 was the first major conference to schedule regular-season night games.

267.

Approximately 16,000 high schools and 900 colleges or universities field football teams in America.

268.

Clemson-South Carolina, Florida State-Miami, and Georgia-Georgia Tech are great college rivalry games in the South.

269.

The "Red River Showdown" featuring the Texas Longhorns and Oklahoma Sooners is a major Southwestern rivalry.

270.

USC and Notre Dame play for the "Jeweled Shillelagh."

271.

The series began in 1926 and was one of college football's first and greatest intersectional rivalries.

272.

A flea flicker is a trick play in which a running back takes a handoff before tossing the ball back to the quarterback to throw a pass.

273.

A goal-line stand occurs when a team's defense keeps the opponent from scoring on several consecutive plays close to the goal line.

274.

Guards are offensive players positioned next to the center on the line of scrimmage.

275.

College and pro football introduced inbound lines or "hash marks" in 1933.

276.

Guards received their name due to "guarding" the center from pre-snap hits and slaps in early football.

277.
A hook and lateral occurs when a receiver runs a hook route, catches the pass, and quickly laterals to a nearby teammate.

278.
"Oskie" is a call made by defensive team members to alert their teammates that an interception has occurred.

279.
The game clock indicates the time remaining in the quarter.

280.
In contrast, the play clock indicates the time left to snap the ball for the current play.

281.

The red zone is a nickname for the area between the defense's 20-yard and goal lines.

282.

Typically, offenses are expected to score after entering the red zone.

283.

Yard after catch or YAC is the yardage a pass receiver gains between the catch and the tackle.

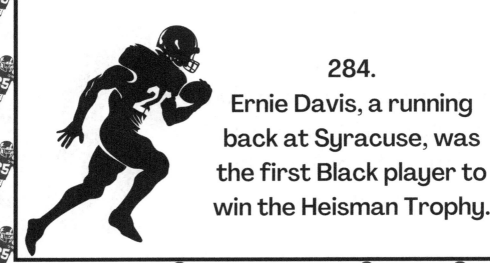

284.

Ernie Davis, a running back at Syracuse, was the first Black player to win the Heisman Trophy.

285.
Charley Trippi was a quintuple threat at Georgia as a runner, passer, receiver, punter, and defensive back.

286.
Texas has produced more NFL players than any other state.

287.
Dave Rimington was a two-time All-American and two-time Academic All-American at Nebraska in the early 1980s.

288.
Named after him, the Rimington Award has been given to the nation's best center since 2000.

289.

College football had a stadium-building boom in the 1920s, with many constructed as memorials to schools.

290.

Football is the favorite sport of 41% of Americans. The next closest sport is baseball at 10%.

291.

Football defenses are named based on the number of defensive linemen and linebackers.

292.

For example, a 43 defense has four defensive linemen and three linebackers.

293.

Don Coryell was an innovative NFL coach who emphasized timing routes and downfield passing.

294.

His San Diego Chargers team led the NFL in passing yardage seven times.

295.

Before 1900, the person holding the ball for place kicks was often called a "placer."

296.

The tradition of letter sweaters evolved from early eastern teams allowing players to keep their jerseys after the season ended.

297.

Team mascots earned their name from an 1880s opera, La Mascotte, about a hired farm girl who brought good luck to a farmer.

298.

"Boosters" are fans of high school and college teams who support their teams financially.

299.

"Trenches" became a slang term for the offensive and defensive lines during WWI.

300.

Harvard's Percy Haughton was the first coach to substitute kickers into the game regularly.

Made in United States
Orlando, FL
07 October 2024

52276736R00046